Europe's Humor Mosaic

Exploring Humor from the North to the South

PUBLISHED BY: Witty Wanderer

Witty Wanderer

Copyright © 2024 Witty Wanderer

All rights reserved. No part of this book may be reproduced, distributed, or transmitted in any form or by any means, including photocopying, recording, or other electronic or mechanical methods, without the prior written permission of the publisher, except in the case of brief quotations embodied in critical reviews and certain other non-commercial uses permitted by copyright law. For permission requests, write to the publisher at the address below.

Table of Contents

Dear reader,..5
Introduction...6
Northern Europe. Dry Wit and Understated Humor.............8
   Denmark..9
      Danish Humor: Wit and Irony..9
   Sweden..14
      Swedish Humor: Dry and Subtle...............................14
   Norway...19
      Norwegian Humor: Playful and Observational..........19
   Finland...24
      Finnish Humor: Minimalist and Dry...........................24
   United Kingdom..29
      British Humor: Clever, Dry, and Self-Deprecating.....29
   Ireland...34
      Irish Humor: Storytelling and Witty Banter................34
   France..38
      French Humor: Intellectual and Satirical...................38
   Belgium...43
      Belgian Humor: Multilingual and Diverse..................43
   The Netherlands...48
      Dutch Humor: Direct and Playful...............................48
   Germany...53
      German Humor: Structured and Unexpected............53
Southern Europe. Passionate and Playful Humor.............58
   Spain..59
      Spanish Humor: Exuberant and Full of Life..............59
   Italy..64
      Italian Humor: Expressive and Gestural....................64
   Portugal..69
      Portuguese Humor: Warm and Reflective.................69
   Greece..74

- Greek Humor: Philosophical and Satirical..................74
- The Balkans. Bold and Unfiltered Humor..........................79
  - Serbia...80
    - Serbian Humor: Sharp and Satirical..........................80
  - Croatia...85
    - Croatian Humor: Playful and Relaxed.......................85
- The Baltic States. Subtle and Sharp Humor.....................90
  - Lithuania...91
    - Lithuanian Humor: Witty and Cultural......................91
  - Latvia...98
    - Latvian Humor: Lively and Observational.................98
  - Estonia..103
    - Estonian Humor: Dry and Subtle............................103
- Eastern Europe. Resilient and Reflective Humor............107
  - Poland...108
    - Polish Humor: Resilient and Ironic..........................108
  - Czech Republic...112
    - Czech Humor: Witty and Satirical...........................112
  - Slovakia...117
    - Slovak Humor: Straightforward and Witty...............117
  - Austria..123
    - Austrian Humor: Sophisticated and Subtle.............123
  - Switzerland..128
    - Swiss Humor: Neutral, Yet Sharp...........................128
  - Hungary...133
    - Hungarian Humor: Rich and Flavorful.....................133
- Conclusion..137
  - Summary of European Humor Styles......................137
  - The Role of Humor in Bridging Cultures.................138
  - Final Thoughts on Humor Across Europe...............139
- Thank You...141

Dear reader,

This book is not merely a collection of jokes, but rather a journey through the unique humor styles of various European countries. From the dry wit of Northern Europe to the playful and passionate humor of the South, this book offers insights into how humor reflects the culture and spirit of each nation. By exploring the wit, satire, and observations that define humor across the continent, you'll gain a deeper appreciation for the diversity and richness of European comedic traditions.

If you enjoy this exploration of Europe's humor, we kindly ask you to leave a positive review on Amazon. Your feedback helps other readers discover and enjoy this book, and we sincerely appreciate your support!

Witty Wanderer

Introduction

Humor is one of the most universal aspects of human experience – we all enjoy a good laugh, but what makes us laugh often varies widely across cultures. Europe, with its rich and diverse history, offers a treasure trove of humor that reflects the unique characteristics of its various nations. From the dry wit of the British to the passionate and gestural humor of the Italians, each European country has its own way of expressing humor.

This book is a journey through the humor of Europe, showcasing the best jokes, anecdotes, and puns from across the continent. It's designed not only to entertain but also to offer insights into how humor reflects cultural values, traditions, and even historical experiences. As you read through these jokes, you'll not only enjoy some good laughs but also gain a deeper understanding of how our European neighbors see themselves and their world.

Humor is also a powerful unifier, transcending language barriers and cultural differences. By exploring the humor of different European countries, we can find common ground and appreciate the diversity of human experience. Whether it's through sharp wit, clever wordplay, or endearing self-deprecation, humor has the power to bring people together and provide a window into the heart of each culture.

So, relax, open the pages of this book, and embark on a delightful journey through European humor. You're bound to find something that makes you smile, and perhaps you'll discover a new perspective on the world through the lens of laughter.

Northern Europe. Dry Wit and Understated Humor

Scandinavian or Northern Europe humor is known for its understated wit, self-deprecation, and often dark comedic elements. In Denmark, Norway, and Sweden, humor reflects the region's values of modesty, simplicity, and a touch of existential reflection. The Scandinavian approach to humor frequently involves poking fun at oneself and addressing life's absurdities with a dry, ironic touch.

Each Scandinavian country has its own flavor of humor, yet they share common traits that emphasize modesty and subtlety. Scandinavian jokes often revolve around the mundane aspects of everyday life, societal norms, and regional quirks, presented with a sense of deadpan delivery.

Denmark

Danish Humor: Wit and Irony

Danish humor is renowned for its wit and irony, often reflecting a deep sense of self-awareness and social commentary. Rooted in a tradition of dry humor and subtlety, Danish jokes frequently employ irony and clever wordplay to provide a humorous take on everyday life and societal norms. The Danish approach to humor is characterized by a balance between lightheartedness and intellectual insight, making it both engaging and thought-provoking.

Danish humor often involves a keen observation of human behavior and societal quirks. It tends to be understated, relying on the audience's ability to pick up on nuances and contextual subtleties. This form of humor can sometimes be a bit self-deprecating, reflecting the Danish value of humility and the cultural tendency to avoid boasting or overt displays of pride.

Popular Danish Jokes and Anecdotes

- A Danish man goes to a new restaurant and asks the waiter, "What do you recommend?" The waiter replies, "Everything is good here, but if you really want something special, try our Danish bacon – it's so good, it might just make you want to move to Denmark!"

- Two Danes are talking about their recent vacation. One says, "We went to Italy and had the best pizza ever!" The other replies, "Really? We had Danish pizza. It was so simple – just cheese and bread. But it made us appreciate the good things in life!"

- A Danish person is asked what makes Denmark such a great place to live. The reply is, "Well, we have the best of everything – good cheese, great beer, and a cozy hygge lifestyle. It's like living in a perpetual state of comfort!"

- A Danish tourist is visiting a small village in Denmark and is amazed by how friendly everyone is. He asks a local, "How do you stay so friendly?" The local answers, "It's easy – we're always smiling because we know it's going to rain tomorrow, so we better enjoy the sun while we can!"

- A Danish farmer is asked why he always wears a hat. He replies, "I wear it because it's practical. When the sun is out, it keeps me cool; when it rains, it keeps me dry. Plus, it's a great conversation starter!"

- A Danish man is telling a story about a fishing trip: "I went out to fish, but the fish weren't biting. So, I had to make my own luck. I threw in a few Danish pastries, and believe me, I caught more fishermen than fish!"

- A Danish child asks his father, "Why do we always have rye bread for breakfast?" The father responds, "Because rye bread is like Danish tradition – simple, hearty, and it sticks with you through thick and thin!"

Traits of Danish Humor

Wit and Irony: Danish humor is often characterized by its wit and use of irony. Jokes and anecdotes typically reflect a sophisticated understanding of human nature and societal norms, providing a humorous perspective on everyday life.

Subtlety: The humor tends to be understated, relying on clever wordplay and nuanced observations. This subtlety requires the audience to be attentive and perceptive, enhancing the overall experience.

Self-Awareness: Danish humor often includes a degree of self-deprecation and social commentary. It reflects the Danish value of humility and a tendency to avoid arrogance or boastfulness.

Cultural Reflection: Danish jokes and anecdotes frequently highlight cultural values and societal quirks. They provide insight into Danish life, traditions, and attitudes, often with a humorous twist.

Balance of Lightheartedness and Insight: Danish humor manages to combine lightheartedness with intellectual depth. It's both entertaining and thought-provoking, offering a balanced view of life's complexities.

Conclusion

Danish humor offers a unique blend of wit, irony, and subtlety that reflects the country's cultural values and social norms. It provides a window into Danish life, highlighting the importance of humor in everyday interactions and societal observations. Whether through clever anecdotes or insightful jokes, Danish humor enriches the cultural landscape with its distinctive style and engaging approach.

Sweden

Swedish Humor: Dry and Subtle

Swedish humor is known for its dry and subtle nature, often characterized by understatement and a wry sense of irony. The Swedish approach to humor typically involves a calm and measured delivery, where the humor is often found in the subtleties and nuances of language and situation. This form of humor can be quite sophisticated, relying on the audience's ability to appreciate the finer details and understated expressions.

In Sweden, humor often mirrors the country's cultural values of modesty and reservedness. It tends to avoid overt displays of emotion or exaggerated reactions, instead opting for a more restrained and reflective style. Swedish jokes frequently highlight the quirks of everyday life, social norms, and the occasional absurdity of human behavior, all delivered with a gentle touch.

Common Swedish Jokes and Observations

- A Swede goes into a bar and orders a beer. The bartender says, "We have a special today: a beer and a shot for the same price!" The Swede thinks for a moment and says, "I'll take the beer and keep the shot – I'm driving!"

- A Swedish man is asked about the weather in Sweden. He replies, "It's always the same: if it's not raining, it's about to. If it's not about to, it's already snowing!"

- Two Swedes are discussing their weekend plans. One says, "I'm going to the countryside to relax." The other replies, "I'm going to the city to do nothing." The first one asks, "Why?" The second one answers, "Because in Sweden, even doing nothing is something!"

- A Swedish tourist is visiting a small village in Sweden and asks a local, "What do you do for fun around here?" The local replies, "Well, we go to the village square, sit quietly, and wait for someone else to start a conversation. It's quite exciting!"

- A Swede is talking about Swedish traditions: "In Sweden, we have a tradition of celebrating Midsummer by dancing around a pole. It's our way of saying, 'We're so happy it's summer, we'll dance around a stick until we can't walk anymore!'"

- A Swedish man is asked how he handles stressful situations. He says, "I just take a deep breath and remember the Swedish motto: 'If you can't fix it, don't worry about it. If you can't worry about it, just enjoy the fika!'"

- A Swede is explaining Swedish punctuality: "In Sweden, we value punctuality so much that if you're even a minute late, you'll have to explain yourself. But don't worry – being early is also considered rude. We just like to keep everyone on their toes!"

Traits of Swedish Humor

Dry and Subtle: Swedish humor is marked by its dryness and subtlety. It often relies on understated delivery and nuanced observations, requiring a keen sense of perception from the audience.

Understatement: The humor frequently involves understatement, where the joke or observation is presented in a calm and composed manner. This approach reflects the Swedish cultural value of modesty and restraint.

Wry Irony: Swedish jokes often feature a wry sense of irony, highlighting the absurdities and quirks of everyday life. This form of humor provides a reflective and often insightful take on common experiences.

Cultural Reflection: Swedish humor reflects the country's cultural values and societal norms. It often addresses the nuances of Swedish life and traditions, offering a humorous perspective on daily routines and social interactions.

Balanced Perspective: Swedish humor provides a balanced perspective on life's challenges and peculiarities. It combines wit and insight with a relaxed and collected approach, making it both engaging and thought-provoking.

Conclusion

Swedish humor offers a unique blend of dry wit and subtlety that reflects the country's cultural values and social norms. Its understated and reflective style provides a window into Swedish life, highlighting the importance of humor in navigating everyday experiences and societal observations. Whether through gentle jokes or nuanced anecdotes, Swedish humor enriches the cultural landscape with its distinctive and engaging approach.

Norway

Norwegian Humor: Playful and Observational

Norwegian humor is often described as playful and observational, reflecting the country's appreciation for both light-hearted fun and keen social insights. This form of humor frequently involves a sense of playfulness and curiosity about human behavior and everyday situations. It's characterized by a casual, friendly approach that engages people through humor that's both entertaining and reflective.

Norwegian jokes and anecdotes often highlight the quirks and peculiarities of life in Norway, from the challenges of navigating its rugged terrain to the unique aspects of its cultural practices. This humor tends to be inclusive, making use of shared experiences and common cultural references to foster a sense of connection and camaraderie among its audience.

Typical Norwegian Jokes and Stories

- A Norwegian man and his friend are talking about hiking in the mountains. The friend asks, "What if we get lost?" The Norwegian replies, "We won't get lost – we'll just find new ways to enjoy the snow!"

- A Norwegian asks a Swede how he manages to stay warm in the winter. The Swede replies, "I just drink hot coffee and wear lots of layers." The Norwegian laughs and says, "In Norway, we just have so much pride that it keeps us warm!"

- A Norwegian and a tourist are discussing Norway's beautiful landscapes. The tourist asks, "How do you describe the fjords?" The Norwegian replies, "Well, imagine a giant Norwegian saying, 'Look at my backyard!'"

- A Norwegian man is asked why he doesn't use a GPS when driving in the countryside. He says, "In Norway, if you get lost, you just follow the fjords until you find your way back. Plus, getting lost is just another way to enjoy nature!"

- Two Norwegians are talking about the long winter nights. One says, "I heard people in other countries use artificial lights to stay awake." The other replies, "In Norway, we embrace the darkness and use it as an excuse to stay in bed all day!"

- A Norwegian is asked about the national sport. He says, "Oh, that's easy – it's called 'trying to stay on the road while avoiding moose!'"

- A tourist in Norway asks a local, "What's the best way to experience Norwegian culture?" The local replies, "Just spend a day with us – we'll take you hiking, show you the northern lights, and explain why we drink so much coffee!"

Traits of Norwegian Humor

Playful and Observational: Norwegian humor is characterized by its playful nature and observational insights. It often focuses on the amusing aspects of daily life and human behavior, providing a light-hearted perspective.

Inclusive: Norwegian jokes and anecdotes are typically inclusive, drawing on common experiences and cultural references to create a sense of connection and shared understanding among the audience.

Friendly and Relaxed: The humor is delivered in a friendly and relaxed manner, making it accessible and engaging. This approach reflects the Norwegian values of community and hospitality.

Cultural Reflection: Norwegian humor often highlights the unique aspects of life in Norway, from its natural beauty to its social customs. It offers a humorous take on the country's traditions and way of life.

Joyful and Engaging: Norwegian humor aims to bring joy and foster a sense of togetherness. It combines playful elements with insightful observations, creating an engaging and entertaining experience for its audience.

Conclusion

Norwegian humor offers a delightful blend of playfulness and observational insight, reflecting the country's cultural values and social norms. Its engaging and inclusive style provides a humorous perspective on the quirks of daily life and the beauty of Norwegian traditions. Through playful jokes and relatable stories, Norwegian humor enriches the cultural landscape with its unique and joyful approach.

Finland

Finnish Humor: Minimalist and Dry

Finnish humor is often described as minimalist and dry, reflecting the country's cultural values of understatement and simplicity. This style of humor tends to be subtle and straightforward, relying on a deadpan delivery and an appreciation for the unembellished aspects of life. Finnish jokes and anecdotes typically feature a pared-down approach, where humor emerges from the ordinary and often mundane aspects of daily existence.

In Finland, humor is frequently characterized by its lack of embellishment. It avoids exaggeration and theatricality, focusing instead on a more restrained and precise form of expression. This minimalist approach allows for a unique form of humor that resonates with the Finnish appreciation for clarity and authenticity. Finnish jokes often involve a clever twist or an ironic observation, delivered with a calm demeanor that reflects the understated nature of Finnish communication.

Finnish Anecdotes and Humor Styles

- A Finnish man is asked why he always wears his winter coat even in the summer. He replies, "In Finland, we don't really have seasons – we just have 'pre-winter' and 'post-winter.'"

- Two Finns are talking about Finnish sauna traditions. One says, "I heard that people in other countries go to the spa for relaxation." The other replies, "In Finland, we go to the sauna to sweat out our problems – it's cheaper and more effective!"

- A tourist in Finland asks a local, "What's the secret to surviving the long, dark winters?" The local says, "Simple – just stay indoors, drink coffee, and remember that summer is just around the corner!"

- A Finnish person is asked why Finns are so quiet. They respond, "We're not quiet – we're just saving our words for when they really matter, like when there's a good sauna session coming up."

- A Finnish man is asked about his opinion on Finnish food. He replies, "Our food is simple and hearty. It's like our weather – you don't need much, just enough to keep you going."

- A Finnish person is asked what they do during the Midnight Sun. They answer, "We stay up late, enjoy the light, and try to explain to our friends why we don't sleep – it's a cultural tradition!"

- Two Finns are discussing their favorite pastime. One says, "I love ice fishing, it's so peaceful." The other replies, "I prefer watching the snow fall while drinking coffee – it's a true Finnish experience!"

Traits of Finnish Humor

Minimalist and Dry: Finnish humor is characterized by its minimalist and dry nature. It often involves a straightforward delivery and an emphasis on simplicity, avoiding embellishment and exaggeration.

Deadpan Delivery: The humor is typically delivered with a deadpan expression, reflecting a calm and composed demeanor. This approach allows for subtlety and nuance in the humor.

Clever Observations: Finnish jokes and anecdotes often feature clever observations about everyday life and human behavior. The humor emerges from the ordinary and mundane, providing a thoughtful and reflective perspective.

Authenticity: Finnish humor values authenticity and clarity. It tends to be genuine and unpretentious, reflecting the cultural appreciation for straightforwardness and simplicity.

Restraint and Understatement: Finnish humor often involves restraint and understatement. It avoids overt emotional displays, focusing instead on a more restrained and precise form of expression.

Conclusion

Finnish humor offers a unique blend of minimalism and dryness that reflects the country's cultural values and communication style. Its straightforward and subtle approach provides a humorous perspective on the everyday and mundane aspects of life. Through clever observations and a calm delivery, Finnish humor enriches the cultural landscape with its distinctive and authentic approach.

Witty Wanderer

Western Europe. A Blend of Charm and Cleverness

Western Europe, with its rich history and cultural diversity, has long been a hub of creativity and wit. The humor in this region is as varied as the countries themselves, ranging from the sharp irony of France to the dry, understated humor of the UK. Western European humor often carries a sense of charm, sophistication, and cleverness, reflecting the region's intellectual traditions and cultural nuances. Each country brings its own distinct flavor to the table, yet they all share an ability to use humor as a tool for both reflection and entertainment. In this chapter, we'll explore the unique comedic styles that make Western Europe a vibrant and essential part of the continent's humor mosaic.

United Kingdom

British Humor: Clever, Dry, and Self-Deprecating

The United Kingdom is famous for its unique sense of humor, characterized by sarcasm, irony, and what's known as "dry humor." Unlike in many cultures, British humor often relies on understatement, subtle wordplay, and a certain level of ambiguity. Many of their jokes appear to be rooted in everyday situations, but there's always a hidden twist or a sense of irony beneath the surface. British humor is also known for its self-deprecation—Brits love to laugh at themselves, particularly when it comes to their quirks and peculiarities.

Although British humor can sometimes seem too subtle or even "cold" to outsiders, those who understand the nuances find it clever and deeply amusing. It requires a keen eye for detail and the ability to read between the lines.

British Jokes

- An Englishman, a Scotsman, and an Irishman walk into a bakery. The Englishman says, "I'll have a scone." The Scotsman says, "I'll have a shortbread." The Irishman looks at the two of them and says, "I'll have a cake. I like to be different."

- A British man is asked what he does when he's stuck in traffic. He replies, "I turn on the radio and listen to the news. It's a great way to find out what everyone else is complaining about."

- An Englishman is on a train and sees a sign saying, "Please offer your seat to elderly or disabled passengers." He thinks to himself, "I've always wanted to be polite, but I'm not sure if I'm elderly or disabled enough!"

- A Scotsman is asked how he can tell if the weather is bad. He replies, "If you can't see the mountain, it's raining. If you can see the mountain, it's going to rain."

- A Brit is asked what he thinks about British weather. He says, "It's not the cold that gets to you, it's the endless rain. But we make the best of it – we complain about it all year long!"

- A Londoner is asked why he loves the city. He responds, "London is great – it's full of history, culture, and people who'll never stop telling you how great London is!"

- A man from Manchester is asked about the best way to deal with British politeness. He says, "Oh, we're very polite, but if someone is too polite, it's usually because they're trying to avoid an awkward conversation about the weather!"

The Traits of British Humor

Sarcasm and Irony: British sarcasm is legendary. It's often delivered so casually that it can be difficult to tell whether the person is joking or being serious. This understated style adds to its charm, especially when the sarcasm is used in mundane, everyday situations.

Dry Humor: Dry humor, or "deadpan," involves saying something ridiculous or witty in a calm, serious tone. The humor lies in the contrast between the serious delivery and the absurdity of the content.

Self-Deprecation: British people are experts in laughing at themselves. They often poke fun at their own flaws, whether it's their stiff upper lip, love for tea, or even their well-known awkwardness. By embracing their imperfections, Brits make light of their identity in a way that's endearing and relatable.

Political Satire: While British humor can be subtle, political satire is a major aspect of their comedic tradition. Shows like "Yes, Minister" and "The Thick of It" have popularized the art of satirizing British politics and government bureaucracy, combining wit with sharp social commentary.

What Makes British Humor Different?

To outsiders, British humor can come across as too subtle or even confusing. Unlike the more boisterous humor found in southern European countries, British jokes often require careful listening and an understanding of the cultural context.

The British often avoid loud laughter or dramatic gestures when delivering jokes. Instead, the humor comes from a quiet observation of life's oddities, delivered in a way that seems so normal, you might miss it if you're not paying attention.

British humor also thrives on breaking down social norms and exposing the silliness of everyday conventions. It's a humor that's sharp but rarely malicious, focusing more on pointing out the absurdity of life's little quirks than outright mocking others.

Ireland

Irish Humor: Storytelling and Witty Banter

Irish humor is renowned for its charm, wit, and storytelling prowess. It often features a delightful mix of self-deprecation, irony, and playful exaggeration. Irish jokes reflect the country's rich tradition of oral storytelling and its ability to find humor in everyday life, from the mundane to the extraordinary.

Irish Jokes

- An Irishman walks into a bakery and asks, "Do you have any fresh bread?" The baker replies, "Yes, we have fresh bread every morning." The Irishman thinks for a moment and says, "Ah, but do you have any that's fresh today?"

- A man from Dublin is asked why he's so cheerful despite the weather. He replies, "Well, you see, it's like this: if you're going to live in Ireland, you might as well enjoy the rain!"

- An Irish farmer is asked what he does to keep the crows away from his crops. He says, "I tell them, 'If you want to eat my corn, you'll have to buy a ticket!'"

- An Irishman is at a pub and is asked if he wants a drink. He replies, "I'm not sure. I was thinking of taking a break from drinking, but then I thought, 'Sure, why start now?'"

- A tourist asks an Irishman for directions. The Irishman says, "Well, if I were you, I wouldn't start from here." When the tourist looks confused, the Irishman adds, "It's the kind of place where it's better to just keep going!"

- Two Irishmen are talking about the weather. One says, "It's so cold, even the cows are shivering." The other replies, "Don't be daft – the cows are fine. It's the people who are freezing!"

- An Irish woman is asked how she stays so positive. She says, "I always look on the bright side. For example, if it's raining, at least I don't have to worry about the sunburn!"

Traits of Irish Humor

Storytelling Tradition: Irish humor is deeply rooted in storytelling. Jokes and anecdotes often feature colorful characters and engaging narratives, reflecting the country's rich oral tradition.

Wit and Irony: Irish humor frequently involves sharp wit and irony. The jokes often play with language and expectations, providing a clever twist or unexpected punchline.

Self-Deprecation: Self-deprecating humor is common in Ireland. People often make light of their own quirks and shortcomings, reflecting a cultural value of humility and self-awareness.

Playful Exaggeration: Irish humor often uses playful exaggeration to highlight the absurdities of everyday life. This approach adds a layer of amusement and charm to the jokes.

Warmth and Affection: Irish humor is known for its warmth and affection. Jokes often celebrate the joy of human connection and the beauty of everyday moments.

How Irish Humor Differs

Irish humor stands out for its combination of storytelling, wit, and affectionate self-deprecation. It often features engaging narratives and clever wordplay, reflecting the country's rich tradition of oral storytelling and its ability to find joy in everyday life.

The humor highlights the cultural values of community and connection, providing a unique and charming perspective on Irish life.

France

French Humor: Intellectual and Satirical

French humor is renowned for its elegance and sophistication, often reflecting the country's rich cultural and intellectual traditions. French jokes and wit frequently involve clever wordplay, puns, and a healthy dose of irony. The French appreciate humor that challenges conventions and pokes fun at social norms, all while maintaining a sense of refinement.

In France, humor can range from the playful and whimsical to the sharply satirical. The French have a long tradition of using humor to critique society and politics, often with a biting wit that reveals deep insights into human nature. French comedy also frequently explores the nuances of human relationships, providing a reflective and often poignant look at life's absurdities.

French Jokes

- A Frenchman walks into a restaurant and orders a meal. When the waiter asks how he wants his steak cooked, the Frenchman replies, "Just tell the chef to think of the meat, then take it out before it gets too attached to the pan."

- A Frenchman is asked what the secret is to a long, happy life. He replies, "Simple: keep a good bottle of wine and a good sense of humor. And remember, you can't have too much of either."

- In Paris, a tourist asks a Frenchman for directions. The Frenchman responds, "Of course, it's easy to get there. Just follow the scent of croissants and you'll eventually find it."

- A Frenchman and a German are arguing about which country has the better cuisine. The Frenchman says, "Well, we have the Eiffel Tower. You have the Brandenburg Gate. But at least we have food that doesn't need a monument to be appreciated!"

- A Parisian is asked what makes the city so special. He replies, "Paris is like a fine wine: it takes time to appreciate. And just like wine, the longer you stay, the more you realize how much you didn't know at first."

- A Frenchman is asked why he's so relaxed. He says, "I take life as it comes. If the cheese is good and the wine is flowing, I'm happy. Everything else can wait."

- A tourist in France is admiring a beautiful old building and asks a Frenchman what it's used for. The Frenchman replies, "Oh, that's just where we keep our history. The real action happens in the cafes!"

Traits of French Humor

Wordplay and Puns: French humor often revolves around clever use of language. The French language itself lends itself to witty wordplay, with many jokes relying on double meanings and puns. This linguistic playfulness is a hallmark of French comedy, delighting in the subtleties and intricacies of the language.

Irony and Satire: French humor is rich in irony, often using it to critique societal norms and political issues. This satirical approach allows the French to address serious topics with a light touch, revealing underlying truths while entertaining.

Sophisticated and Elegant: French humor maintains a level of sophistication that reflects the country's cultural values. Jokes and comedic situations often involve a certain degree of refinement and wit, distinguishing them from more straightforward or slapstick forms of comedy.

Romantic and Philosophical: French humor frequently explores themes of romance and philosophy. It's not uncommon for French jokes to delve into existential questions or to playfully examine the nature of love and relationships.

How French Humor Differs

French humor is characterized by its intellectualism and subtlety. Unlike some cultures that favor more overt and boisterous forms of comedy, French jokes often require a degree of cultural and linguistic understanding. The humor can be both cerebral and whimsical, reflecting the French appreciation for both high culture and everyday absurdities.

The French are adept at using humor to navigate complex social and political landscapes, often employing satire to make pointed observations about society. This ability to combine elegance with critique is what sets French humor apart from other traditions, offering a unique perspective that is both insightful and entertaining.

Belgium

Belgian Humor: Multilingual and Diverse

Belgian humor is characterized by its multilingual and diverse nature, reflecting the country's complex cultural landscape. With three official languages—Dutch, French, and German—Belgium is a melting pot of linguistic and cultural influences, which is vividly reflected in its humor. This diversity creates a rich tapestry of comedic styles, blending elements from different cultures and regions.

Belgian humor often involves a mix of languages and cultural references, making it uniquely varied and multifaceted. Jokes and anecdotes in Belgium can span across different linguistic communities, incorporating the distinct flavors of Dutch, French, and German humor. This multilingual aspect of Belgian humor allows for a broad range of comedic expressions, from witty wordplay to satirical observations, all contributing to a vibrant and inclusive sense of humor.

Belgian Jokes and Anecdotes

- A Belgian walks into a chocolate shop and asks for the best chocolate they have. The shopkeeper points to a box and says, "This one's very special; it's made with Belgian cocoa." The Belgian replies, "Well, it better be, because that's the only kind I trust!"

- A Belgian and a Frenchman are debating which country has the better beer. The Belgian says, "We have so many varieties that even our beer has its own beer!"

- In Brussels, a tourist asks a Belgian why the city is famous for its waffles. The Belgian replies, "It's simple. Waffles are like us: a little bit of everything, and always with a bit of sweet surprise."

- A Belgian is asked how he stays so calm in traffic. He says, "I don't worry about the traffic. I just remember that the longer I'm stuck, the longer I can enjoy my favorite Belgian radio stations."

- A Belgian is talking about his job and says, "I work in a very specialized field: chocolate engineering. My job is to make sure every piece of chocolate is perfectly engineered to bring joy."

- Two Belgians are discussing their weekend plans. One says, "I'm going to the beach." The other asks, "Which one?" The first replies, "The one with the best chocolate shops, of course!"

- A Belgian is at a party and someone asks him for the secret to making the perfect beer. He replies, "It's all about balance. A little bit of hops, a little bit of malt, and a lot of patience. And of course, a bit of Belgian charm!"

Traits of Belgian Humor

Multilingual: Belgian humor often incorporates elements from multiple languages, reflecting the country's linguistic diversity. This multilingual aspect adds depth and variety to the humor.

Diverse: Belgian humor is diverse, drawing from the different cultural influences within the country. It includes a range of comedic styles, from witty wordplay to satirical observations.

Inclusive: The humor tends to be inclusive, bridging cultural and linguistic gaps. It reflects the multicultural nature of Belgium and its ability to blend various comedic traditions.

Cultural Reflection: Belgian jokes and anecdotes frequently highlight the country's unique cultural landscape. They offer a humorous perspective on Belgian life, traditions, and stereotypes.

Playful and Engaging: Belgian humor is playful and engaging, often using humor as a way to connect with others and navigate the complexities of a multilingual society.

Conclusion

Belgian humor offers a rich and diverse blend of multilingual and cultural influences, reflecting the country's unique linguistic and cultural landscape. Its ability to integrate elements from Dutch, French, and German humor creates a vibrant and inclusive comedic style. Through playful jokes and engaging anecdotes, Belgian humor provides a window into the complexities and joys of life in

Belgium, celebrating the country's diverse and multifaceted nature.

The Netherlands

Dutch Humor: Direct and Playful

Dutch humor is known for its directness, straightforwardness, and often irreverent tone. It's characterized by a blend of sharp wit, self-irony, and a penchant for satire. In the Netherlands, humor frequently involves a no-nonsense approach to social norms and a willingness to poke fun at various aspects of life, from bureaucracy to personal habits.

Dutch jokes often play on the country's unique social dynamics and cultural traits, providing a humorous look at everyday experiences. The humor is typically candid and unembellished, reflecting the Dutch value of openness and honesty.

Dutch Jokes

- A Dutchman is walking through the countryside when he sees a farmer struggling with a stubborn cow. He offers to help and, after a bit of effort, manages to get the cow back in the barn. The farmer thanks him and says, "You must be very strong!" The Dutchman replies, "No, just very persistent. In the Netherlands, we're all used to getting things done, even if it takes a little push!"

- A Dutch tourist is in a foreign country and sees a sign that says "Dutch Pancakes Served Here." Excited, he goes in and asks, "Do you have real Dutch pancakes?" The waiter replies, "Of course! They're just like the ones you'd have at home, only without the windmills."

- A Dutchman is asked about his favorite hobby. He replies, "I love riding my bike. It's the perfect way to get around, and if it rains, I just put on my raincoat and keep going. In the Netherlands, we don't let a little weather stop us!"

- A Dutch couple is planning their vacation and the husband says, "I want to go somewhere sunny and warm." The wife replies, "Why don't we just stay home and enjoy our tulips? They're always in bloom and they never complain about the weather."

- A Dutchman is discussing his diet and says, "I eat a lot of cheese. It's a staple here. We have so many varieties that sometimes I think we should have a cheese museum!" His friend responds, "We do have one. It's called the Cheese Market!"

- A tourist in Amsterdam asks a local for directions. The local says, "It's easy! Just follow the canals. They'll lead you to where you want to go. And if you get lost, just look for the nearest café. We Dutch are never far from a good cup of coffee!"

- A Dutchman is at a party and someone asks him if he likes the Dutch weather. He replies, "I don't mind it. In fact, I think the weather here is like our cheese—diverse and interesting. You just have to appreciate it for what it is!"

Traits of Dutch Humor

Direct and Candid: Dutch humor is characterized by its directness. Jokes and comedic situations are often straightforward and unfiltered, reflecting the Dutch value of honesty and openness.

Self-Irony: The Dutch often use self-irony in their humor, poking fun at their own quirks and cultural traits. This self-deprecating humor provides a way to address imperfections with a sense of light-heartedness.

Satirical and Critical: Dutch humor frequently includes satire, especially when addressing social and political issues. This critical edge allows for commentary on various aspects of society while entertaining.

Pragmatic and Practical: Dutch humor often reflects a pragmatic approach to life. Jokes frequently focus on practical matters, emphasizing the no-nonsense attitude that characterizes Dutch culture.

Everyday Observations: Dutch humor often centers on everyday life and common experiences. The jokes are relatable and highlight the humorous aspects of routine activities and social interactions.

How Dutch Humor Differs

Dutch humor is notable for its straightforward and unembellished nature. It often involves a candid approach to social norms and personal habits, delivered with a sharp wit and a touch of irreverence. Unlike more subtle or elaborate forms of humor, Dutch jokes are typically direct and practical, reflecting the country's cultural emphasis on honesty and efficiency.

The humor also includes a significant amount of self-irony and satire, allowing for both self-reflection and social critique. This blend of directness, practicality, and critical humor provides a unique perspective on Dutch life and culture.

Germany

German Humor: Structured and Unexpected

German humor is often described as straightforward and pragmatic, reflecting the country's no-nonsense approach to life. It's known for its blend of dry wit, clever wordplay, and a fondness for self-deprecation. Germans tend to appreciate humor that is direct and unpretentious, often highlighting the absurdities of everyday life with a touch of sarcasm.

German jokes frequently revolve around practical situations, social norms, and the quirks of human behavior. There is a notable fondness for "Schadenfreude" – the pleasure derived from another's misfortune – which is often employed in a light-hearted and good-natured manner. German humor also has a strong tradition of satire, using humor to comment on social and political issues with a sharp edge.

German Jokes

- A German man walks into a bar and orders a beer. The bartender asks, "Would you like a light or dark beer?" The German replies, "I'll have a light beer, please. After all, we Germans like our beers like we like our efficiency—simple and straightforward!"

- A German engineer and a French chef are having a conversation. The chef says, "In France, we believe in using the finest ingredients to make the best food." The engineer responds, "In Germany, we use precision and order to ensure everything works perfectly. For example, our trains run on time and our sausages are precisely measured!"

- Two Germans are at a train station waiting for their train. One says, "It's so punctual, it's almost too perfect." The other replies, "Yes, but remember, punctuality is the art of waiting. We Germans have mastered the art of being on time!"

- A German tourist is visiting New York and is amazed by the chaos. He says, "In Germany, we have a saying: 'Order and cleanliness are the hallmarks of a good society.' Here, it seems like everyone is trying to prove that disorder can be just as effective!"

- A German is asked about his favorite holiday. He says, "I love Oktoberfest. It's the only time when we combine our love for beer with our passion for organization. It's the perfect blend of fun and efficiency!"

- A German student is taking a test and finds a tricky question. He thinks for a moment and writes, "The answer is: 'It depends on how you approach it.' In Germany, we believe that with the right method and diligence, any problem can be solved!"

- A German and a Dutchman are having a conversation about their countries. The Dutchman says, "In the Netherlands, we're known for our windmills and canals." The German responds, "In Germany, we're known for our cars and precision. But I guess we both appreciate the importance of keeping things running smoothly!"

Traits of German Humor

Pragmatic and Direct: German humor is known for its practical nature. Jokes often focus on everyday situations, presenting them with a blend of irony and straightforwardness. This direct approach reflects the German value placed on efficiency and clarity.

Dry Wit: Germans have a penchant for dry humor, where the comedy often lies in the understated delivery of a joke. The humor is typically subtle, requiring a bit of thought to fully appreciate.

Self-Deprecation: Germans are often willing to laugh at themselves. This self-deprecating humor is used to highlight their own quirks and shortcomings, providing a way to address flaws with a sense of humor.

Satirical and Critical: German humor frequently includes a satirical edge, particularly in its commentary on societal norms and political issues. This form of humor serves as both entertainment and critique, offering a way to question and examine social realities.

Schadenfreude: The concept of deriving pleasure from others' misfortunes is a recurring theme in German jokes.

However, this is typically done in a light-hearted manner, reflecting a cultural tendency to find humor in life's little challenges.

How German Humor Differs

German humor is often more structured and less flamboyant compared to some other European traditions. It emphasizes practicality and directness, with a focus on clear and concise delivery. The humor is less likely to rely on elaborate setups or emotional outbursts and more on clever observations and practical jokes.

The German approach to humor reflects the country's broader cultural values, including a strong sense of order, efficiency, and a certain seriousness. This does not mean the humor is lacking in warmth or creativity; rather, it is expressed in a manner that aligns with the German way of engaging with the world.

Southern Europe. Passionate and Playful Humor

In Southern Europe, humor is infused with the same warmth, passion, and energy that characterize the region's vibrant cultures. From the lively wit of Spain and the playful charm of Italy to the clever wordplay of Portugal and the spirited satire of Greece, humor in this part of Europe is as bold and expressive as its people. Southern Europeans often use humor to navigate life's challenges, finding joy in the everyday and laughter in the face of adversity. In this chapter, we'll dive into the rich and dynamic humor of Southern Europe, where stories, jokes, and anecdotes are told with heart and soul, reflecting the region's love for life and connection to tradition.

Spain

Spanish Humor: Exuberant and Full of Life

Spanish humor is as vibrant and passionate as the culture it springs from. It often reflects the country's rich traditions, lively festivals, and regional diversity. Spanish jokes tend to be animated and full of energy, incorporating elements of theatricality, wordplay, and social commentary.

Spain's humor is deeply rooted in its cultural practices and historical experiences, from the exuberant celebrations of local fiestas to the sharp wit of its literary tradition. Spanish comedy often tackles everyday life, politics, and the quirks of regional identities with a sense of playfulness and irony.

Spanish Jokes

- A Spaniard walks into a tapas bar and orders a drink. The bartender asks, "Would you like some tapas with that?" The Spaniard replies, "Of course! In Spain, we believe that the real meal starts after the drink!"

- A tourist asks a Spaniard about the secret to making paella. The Spaniard says, "The secret is in the patience. You must wait for the perfect moment when the rice is just right and the saffron is infused. But remember, in Spain, patience is just another way of enjoying the meal!"

- A Spaniard is asked why he is always late. He says, "In Spain, time is like a flexible concept. We like to savor life's moments, even if it means arriving fashionably late!"

- Two friends are talking about their weekend plans. One says, "I'm going to watch a bullfight." The other asks, "Why?" The first replies, "Because nothing says Spanish tradition like a good bullfight, and besides, it's a lot of drama and excitement!"

- A Spaniard goes to the doctor and says, "Doctor, I'm feeling really tired." The doctor asks, "How much sleep are you getting?" The Spaniard replies, "Not much. I'm too busy enjoying the fiesta and the late-night socializing!"

- A Spaniard and a Frenchman are discussing their cuisines. The Frenchman says, "In France, we enjoy fine dining and gourmet meals." The Spaniard responds, "In Spain, we believe in enjoying every meal with friends and family, and adding a bit of flair to it. It's not just about the food, but the experience!"

- A Spaniard is asked about his favorite holiday. He says, "I love La Tomatina. There's nothing like a massive tomato fight to remind us that life is meant to be fun and messy!"

Traits of Spanish Humor

Energetic and Expressive: Spanish humor is known for its dynamic and spirited delivery. Jokes and comedic situations often involve lively expressions and animated storytelling, reflecting the high energy and zest of Spanish culture.

Wordplay and Puns: Spanish humor frequently involves clever wordplay and puns. The Spanish language is rich with opportunities for linguistic play, and this is a common feature in jokes and comedic dialogues.

Social Commentary: Spanish jokes often touch on social and political themes. This form of humor serves as a way to comment on and critique societal norms and political issues, often with a humorous twist.

Regional Differences: Spain's diverse regional cultures contribute to a variety of humor styles. Jokes can vary widely depending on the region, reflecting local customs, traditions, and stereotypes.

Celebratory Spirit: Spanish humor often embraces the celebratory aspects of life. Whether through festivals, food, or family gatherings, the humor highlights the joy and exuberance that characterize Spanish life.

How Spanish Humor Differs

Spanish humor stands out for its vibrancy and emotional expressiveness. It often involves a high degree of theatricality and animation, making the delivery as entertaining as the content. Unlike more reserved humor styles, Spanish jokes are frequently bold and lively, reflecting the cultural importance placed on celebration and social interaction.

The humor is deeply intertwined with the country's cultural practices, from festive celebrations to regional diversity. This connection to cultural traditions adds layers of meaning to the jokes, making them resonate with the nuances of Spanish life.

Italy

Italian Humor: Expressive and Gestural

Italian humor is renowned for its vibrancy and emotional expressiveness, reflecting the passionate nature of Italian culture. It is often characterized by lively gestures, dramatic flair, and a deep appreciation for the absurdities of life. Italian jokes frequently involve physical comedy, clever wordplay, and affectionate mockery of societal norms and personal habits.

Humor in Italy is a vital part of social interaction, often used to diffuse tension, build camaraderie, and highlight the quirks of daily life. The Italian sense of humor can be both playful and sophisticated, frequently intertwining with the country's rich tradition of art, literature, and theater.

Italian Jokes

- An Italian man is asked why he always talks with his hands. He replies, "In Italy, it's not just what you say but how you say it. The hands help to express the passion and emotions behind the words!"

- A tourist in Rome asks an Italian, "How do you tell a good pizza from a bad one?" The Italian replies, "A good pizza is like a good friend—it's simple, reliable, and always makes you happy. If it's overly complicated, it's probably not worth your time!"

- A waiter in an Italian restaurant is asked how he manages to stay so calm despite the busy hours. He responds, "In Italy, we have a saying: 'La vita è bella,' which means 'Life is beautiful.' Even during the busiest times, we remember to enjoy the moment and savor the experience!"

- An Italian is asked why Italians are so passionate about their coffee. He says, "Italians don't just drink coffee; they experience it. Each cup is a small ritual, a moment to savor and enjoy life's simple pleasures!"

- An Italian man is asked why he's always so late. He replies, "In Italy, we have a saying: 'Dove c'è vita, c'è speranza'—where there is life, there is hope. So, if I'm late, it's because I'm busy enjoying life's moments!"

- Two friends are discussing their favorite Italian foods. One says, "I love pasta!" The other replies, "Pasta is great, but nothing beats a well-made risotto. It's like comparing a good friend to a true soulmate—both are great, but one has a special place in your heart!"

- An Italian family is asked why they have such elaborate dinners. The Italian responds, "In Italy, meals are more than just food—they are about bringing people together, sharing stories, and creating memories. The food is just the excuse for a great time!"

Traits of Italian Humor

Expressive and Physical: Italian humor often incorporates physical gestures and expressive body language. This lively approach adds an extra layer of comedy, making interactions more engaging and animated.

Wordplay and Puns: Italians enjoy playing with words, creating puns and clever twists on language. This wordplay is often used to add humor to everyday conversations and situations.

Romantic and Theatrical: Humor in Italy frequently reflects the country's romantic and theatrical traditions. Jokes and comedic scenarios often involve exaggerated emotions and dramatic flair, celebrating the joy and absurdity of life.

Affectionate Mockery: Italians have a fondness for gently poking fun at each other's habits and cultural quirks. This affectionate humor highlights the close-knit nature of Italian society and the ability to laugh at oneself.

Food and Family: Food and family are central themes in Italian humor. Jokes often revolve around meals, culinary traditions, and the lively dynamics of family gatherings.

How Italian Humor Differs

Italian humor stands out for its emotional intensity and physical expressiveness. Unlike more reserved humor styles, Italian jokes are delivered with passion and often involve lively gestures. The humor tends to be more interpersonal and situational, reflecting the importance of personal connections and the enjoyment of life's pleasures.

The focus on food, family, and romance in Italian humor underscores the cultural values that prioritize relationships and the joy of living. Italian humor is less about subtlety and more about embracing the full spectrum of human experience with enthusiasm and warmth.

Portugal

Portuguese Humor: Warm and Reflective

Portuguese humor is rich in warmth, characterized by its gentle irony, clever wordplay, and a deep connection to the country's cultural and historical heritage. It reflects the Portuguese appreciation for subtlety and a unique blend of melancholy and joy. Portuguese jokes often involve playful teasing, whimsical stories, and a fondness for puns and double entendres.

Humor in Portugal often delves into everyday life, including the idiosyncrasies of local customs and the quirks of regional identities. The Portuguese sense of humor is known for its ability to find lightness in both the mundane and the profound aspects of life.

Portuguese Jokes

- A Portuguese man is asked how he manages to stay so calm and relaxed. He replies, "In Portugal, we have a saying: 'Devagar se vai ao longe'—slowly, you get far. We believe in taking our time and enjoying the journey!"

- A tourist in Lisbon asks a local, "What's the best way to enjoy a traditional Portuguese meal?" The local replies, "The best way is to start with a glass of port wine, savor the flavors of each dish, and remember that the meal is as much about the company as it is about the food!"

- A Portuguese woman is asked why she always adds so much garlic to her dishes. She says, "Garlic is like a little bit of sunshine in our food. It adds flavor and warmth, just like how we like to bring warmth and cheer into our lives!"

- A Portuguese man is asked how he manages to keep his garden so beautiful. He replies, "In Portugal, we believe that if you take care of something with love, it will thrive. The same goes for our gardens—they reflect the care and attention we give them!"

- A waiter in a Portuguese restaurant is asked what makes Portuguese cuisine so special. He responds,

"It's the love and tradition that goes into every dish. From the simplest seafood to the most elaborate feasts, Portuguese food is all about celebrating life and good company!"

- An old Portuguese saying goes, "Quem espera sempre alcança"—who waits always achieves. A local explains, "This means that patience and persistence are key to success. Whether you're waiting for the right moment or a perfect dish, good things come to those who wait!"

- A Portuguese man is asked why he always seems to have time for a chat. He replies, "In Portugal, we value the moments we spend with friends and family. Life is too short to rush—enjoying a good conversation is as important as anything else!"

Traits of Portuguese Humor

Gentle Irony: Portuguese humor often features a gentle irony that highlights the subtleties of human behavior and social norms. This form of humor is both light-hearted and reflective, offering a nuanced view of life.

Wordplay and Puns: Clever wordplay and puns are common in Portuguese jokes. The language's rich vocabulary provides ample opportunities for humorous twists and double meanings.

Warm and Affectionate: Portuguese humor tends to be warm and affectionate, reflecting the country's cultural emphasis on close relationships and community. Jokes often have a playful and endearing quality.

Everyday Observations: Humor in Portugal frequently revolves around everyday life and local customs. Jokes highlight the quirks of daily routines and regional habits, making the humor relatable and grounded.

Melancholic Joy: Portuguese humor often blends a sense of melancholy with joy. This combination reflects a cultural ability to find humor in life's challenges while appreciating its moments of happiness.

How Portuguese Humor Differs

Portuguese humor is distinguished by its subtlety and warmth. It often involves gentle irony and affectionate teasing, reflecting the country's cultural values of community and connection. Unlike more overt forms of comedy, Portuguese jokes are typically delivered with a sense of grace and an appreciation for the complexities of life.

The humor frequently incorporates elements of wordplay and local traditions, offering a unique perspective on Portuguese life. It combines a sense of melancholy with joy, providing a balanced and reflective view of the human experience.

Greece

Greek Humor: Philosophical and Satirical

Greek humor is deeply intertwined with the country's rich historical and cultural heritage. Known for its lively storytelling, wit, and philosophical depth, Greek humor often reflects the values of community, tradition, and a playful engagement with life's challenges. It combines ancient traditions with modern sensibilities, resulting in a distinctive and engaging comedic style.

Greek jokes frequently involve clever wordplay, historical references, and a touch of irreverence. They often highlight the cultural quirks of Greek society and celebrate the country's legendary hospitality and warmth.

Greek Jokes

- A Greek man is asked why Greeks are always so passionate about their food. He replies, "In Greece, food is more than just a meal; it's an experience. We put our heart and soul into our cooking because we

- believe that sharing a meal is a way of sharing love and joy!"
- A Greek tourist asks a local why Greek coffee is so strong. The local answers, "Greek coffee is strong because we believe in starting the day with a strong kick! Plus, it gives us the energy to enjoy long conversations and the pleasures of life!"
- A Greek woman is asked how she manages to cook such amazing Greek dishes. She says, "It's all about using fresh, local ingredients and adding a touch of Greek philosophy. Every dish is a reflection of our culture, and we put love and care into every recipe!"
- A Greek man is asked why Greek myths are so fascinating. He replies, "Greek myths are like mirrors reflecting our values and beliefs. They are full of drama, heroism, and lessons about life, just like our own experiences!"
- An American tourist in Greece asks a local why Greeks love to dance so much. The local answers, "Dancing is a way for us to celebrate life and express our joy. In Greece, we believe that dancing

brings people together and keeps the spirit of our traditions alive!"

- A Greek philosopher is asked about the secret to happiness. He replies, "The secret to happiness is simple: enjoy the little things in life, savor your food, cherish your friends and family, and always stay true to yourself. Life is too short to worry about the small stuff!"

- A Greek man is asked why Greek mythology is so influential. He responds, "Greek mythology has shaped our culture and thinking for centuries. It teaches us about the human condition, the nature of gods, and the importance of living a virtuous life. It's a legacy that continues to inspire us today!"

Traits of Greek Humor

Storytelling Tradition: Greek humor is often expressed through lively storytelling. These stories are rich in detail, featuring colorful characters and humorous situations that reflect the country's oral tradition.

Clever Wordplay: Greek jokes frequently involve clever wordplay and puns. The language's expressive nature provides ample opportunities for linguistic humor and witty remarks.

Philosophical Depth: Greek humor sometimes incorporates philosophical reflections, drawing on the country's rich intellectual heritage. Jokes may touch on existential themes or offer insights into the human condition.

Cultural Quirks: Humor in Greece often highlights the unique aspects of Greek culture and society. Jokes may focus on local customs, regional habits, and the idiosyncrasies of daily life.

Warmth and Hospitality: Greek humor reflects the country's emphasis on hospitality and community. Jokes often celebrate the joy of sharing meals and experiences with others, highlighting the importance of relationships and connection.

How Greek Humor Differs

Greek humor is characterized by its blend of storytelling, wit, and philosophical depth. It often incorporates elements of ancient traditions and modern life, creating a rich and engaging comedic style. Unlike more direct forms of humor, Greek jokes frequently use narrative and wordplay to explore cultural and existential themes.

The humor reflects the country's values of community, tradition, and warmth. It provides a unique perspective on Greek life, celebrating the joy and complexity of human experience through a combination of ancient wisdom and contemporary insights.

The Balkans. Bold and Unfiltered Humor

Balkan humor, especially from countries like Serbia and Croatia, is renowned for its sharp wit and unfiltered nature. This humor often draws on the region's complex history and cultural richness, reflecting a deep-seated resilience and a distinctive, irreverent spirit. In Serbia, humor frequently involves clever observations and satirical takes on daily life, portraying both the absurdities and the harsh realities with a boldness that challenges conventions.

In Croatia, humor is characterized by playful exaggerations and a keen sense of irony, highlighting the contrasts between rural and urban experiences. This approach not only entertains but also offers insights into Croatian traditions and social dynamics. Across the Balkans, humor serves as a way to navigate and make light of life's challenges, showcasing the region's unique ability to blend resilience with a profound sense of comedic timing.

Serbia

Serbian Humor: Sharp and Satirical

Serbian humor is known for its sharpness and satirical edge, reflecting a deep tradition of using humor as a means of social commentary and critique. This form of humor often involves clever wordplay, irony, and a keen observation of societal and political issues. Serbian jokes and anecdotes frequently address the nuances of everyday life and the complexities of social dynamics, using humor to provide insight and provoke thought.

The satirical nature of Serbian humor allows for a bold and sometimes irreverent approach to addressing topics that might otherwise be considered sensitive. It's characterized by a willingness to challenge norms and question authority, making it both entertaining and intellectually stimulating. Serbian humor often walks a fine line between humor and criticism, offering a unique perspective on the country's cultural and social landscape.

Serbian Jokes and Observations

- A Serbian is asked why he's always late. He replies, "In Serbia, we have a special time zone called 'Serbian Time'—everything runs a bit late, but it's always worth the wait!"
- A Serb and a Croatian are arguing about whose country has the best coffee. The Serb says, "Our coffee is strong and wakes you up instantly!" The Croatian responds, "That's nothing! Our coffee is so good, it keeps you awake to enjoy the whole day!"
- A Serbian man goes to a doctor and complains about a headache. The doctor says, "You need to relax more!" The man replies, "I don't have time for that. I'm too busy relaxing with my friends and enjoying life!"
- A Serbian tourist in New York asks a local where to find good food. The New Yorker says, "You're in New York! We have everything!" The Serbian responds, "Great! I'll start with a Serbian restaurant, and if I can't find one, I'll settle for some New York pizza."

- A Serbian man is asked what makes Serbian music unique. He says, "Serbian music is full of passion and rhythm! It's the heartbeat of our culture and brings people together to celebrate life!"

- A Serbian is asked how he feels about the weather in winter. He says, "Winter in Serbia is like a long family gathering—sometimes a bit cold, but full of warmth and comfort when you're with the ones you love."

- A Serb is asked why he always invites so many people to his house. He replies, "In Serbia, we believe that the more, the merrier! And besides, the more friends we have, the more laughter and stories we share!"

Traits of Serbian Humor

Sharp and Satirical: Serbian humor is known for its sharpness and satirical edge. It often involves clever wordplay and irony, using humor to comment on social and political issues.

Bold and Irreverent: The humor frequently challenges norms and questions authority. It's characterized by a bold and sometimes irreverent approach, providing a unique perspective on serious topics.

Observational: Serbian jokes and anecdotes often feature keen observations about everyday life and societal dynamics. This observational humor offers insight into the complexities of Serbian culture.

Social Commentary: Serbian humor serves as a form of social commentary, using satire and wit to address and critique various aspects of society. It's both entertaining and thought-provoking.

Engaging and Provocative: Serbian humor is engaging and provocative, combining humor with critical reflection. It stimulates thought and discussion, making it an integral part of the cultural discourse.

Conclusion

Serbian humor offers a distinctive blend of sharpness and satire, reflecting the country's tradition of using humor as a tool for social commentary and critique. Its ability to address serious topics with wit and cleverness provides a unique perspective on Serbian life and culture. Through bold jokes and insightful observations, Serbian humor enriches the cultural landscape with its engaging and thought-provoking approach.

Croatia

Croatian Humor: Playful and Relaxed

Croatian humor is celebrated for its playful and relaxed nature, embodying a light-hearted approach to life's everyday moments and social interactions. This style of humor often features a blend of wit, charm, and warmth, reflecting the Croatian appreciation for good-natured fun and easygoing social interactions. The humor is typically characterized by a sense of ease and informality, making it accessible and enjoyable for a wide audience.

Croatian jokes and anecdotes often revolve around daily life, local customs, and the quirks of social behavior. They highlight the ability of Croatians to find humor in both ordinary and extraordinary situations, often using self-deprecation and light-hearted teasing to bring out the comedic elements of various scenarios. The playful nature of Croatian humor makes it a central part of social gatherings and casual conversations, fostering a sense of community and shared enjoyment.

Croatian Jokes and Stories

- A Croatian man goes to a doctor and says, "Doctor, I keep forgetting things!" The doctor asks, "How long has this been going on?" The man replies, "How long has what been going on?"
- Two Croatians are discussing their favorite foods. One says, "I love Croatian cuisine because it's simple and delicious!" The other replies, "I agree, but sometimes I wish it were more complex—like trying to understand our traffic laws!"
- A Croatian fisherman is asked what makes Croatian fish so tasty. He replies, "It's the secret seasoning we use—lots of fresh air, a little sea salt, and a big catch of patience!"
- A Croatian tourist is lost in Paris and asks a local for directions. The Parisian says, "You're in Paris! Just follow your nose!" The Croatian responds, "Great! I'll follow the smell of fresh pastries and hope it leads me to the Eiffel Tower!"
- A Croatian man is having a conversation with a friend about the weather. The friend says, "It's so hot

outside!" The man replies, "Don't worry, it's only Croatian summer—just stay hydrated and enjoy the sun!"

- A Croatian is asked how they stay so relaxed. They say, "In Croatia, we have a saying: 'Life is too short to worry.' So we spend our time enjoying the beach, the wine, and the company of good friends."

- A Croatian grandmother is asked about her secret to a long life. She says, "It's simple: always eat well, laugh often, and don't let the small things bother you. And never forget to dance to traditional music whenever you get the chance!"

Traits of Croatian Humor

Playful and Relaxed: Croatian humor is characterized by its playful and relaxed nature. It focuses on enjoying life and finding humor in everyday situations with a light-hearted approach.

Witty and Charming: The humor often involves witty remarks and charming observations. It reflects the Croatian ability to bring a sense of fun and enjoyment to social interactions.

Self-Deprecating: Croatian jokes frequently include self-deprecation and light-hearted teasing. This form of humor helps to create a friendly and inclusive atmosphere.

Cultural Reflection: Croatian humor often highlights local customs and social behaviors, offering a humorous perspective on Croatian life and traditions.

Community and Connection: Humor plays a central role in fostering a sense of community and connection. It's an important part of social gatherings and casual conversations, enhancing the enjoyment of shared experiences.

Conclusion

Croatian humor offers a delightful blend of playfulness and relaxation, reflecting the country's appreciation for light-hearted fun and good-natured social interactions. Its focus on everyday moments and local customs provides a warm and engaging perspective on Croatian life. Through witty jokes and charming anecdotes, Croatian humor enriches the cultural landscape with its easygoing and inclusive approach.

The Baltic States. Subtle and Sharp Humor

The Baltic States—Lithuania, Latvia, and Estonia—each have their unique sense of humor, yet they share some common traits shaped by their shared history and regional experiences. The humor in these countries often combines wit, irony, and a playful approach to their shared cultural and historical contexts.

Lithuania

Lithuanian Humor: Witty and Cultural

Lithuanian humor is characterized by its wit and cultural depth, reflecting the country's rich traditions and sharp observational skills. This style of humor often blends clever wordplay with cultural references, providing a humorous yet insightful perspective on Lithuanian life. Lithuanian jokes and anecdotes frequently draw from local customs, historical events, and everyday experiences, offering a unique window into the country's cultural landscape.

The wit in Lithuanian humor is often expressed through clever turns of phrase and ironic observations, making it both entertaining and thought-provoking. It reflects a deep appreciation for both the nuances of language and the complexities of social interactions. Lithuanian humor tends to be both reflective and playful, balancing sharpness with a sense of cultural pride and identity.

Lithuanian Jokes and Anecdotes

- A Lithuanians' logic: A Lithuanian is asked why he always buys two of everything. He replies, "Well, you never know if the first one will break. And if it doesn't, at least I'll have a spare for when I need it!"

- Regional rivalry: A man from Vilnius and a man from Kaunas are arguing. The Vilnius man says, "In Vilnius, we have everything!" The Kaunas man replies, "That's nice, but in Kaunas, we have the best of everything!"

- The neighbor's cow: A Lithuanian farmer is asked how he deals with his neighbor's cow that keeps wandering into his field. He says, "I told my neighbor, 'If you can't keep your cow at home, at least make sure it eats the weeds!'"

- Tourist's question: A foreign tourist asks a Lithuanian, "What's the best way to experience Lithuania?" The Lithuanian replies, "Visit during a festival, try some traditional food, and make sure to get lost a few times—it's the best way to find your way around!"

- The Lithuanian's philosophy: A Lithuanian is asked why he doesn't get stressed. He says, "In Lithuania, we believe in 'live and let live.' If you can't fix it, why worry? Instead, enjoy a good meal and a glass of beer."

- Traditional advice: A Lithuanian grandmother is asked for her secret to a long life. She says, "It's simple: work hard, enjoy your family, and always have some good stories to tell!"

- Wisdom of the countryside: A city dweller visits a Lithuanian village and asks an old man what the secret to happiness is. The old man replies, "Happiness is like a good farm—easy to tend, but hard to build. It comes from knowing how to enjoy the simple things in life."

- The wolf asks the rabbit: Rabbit, did you go hunting today?
  The rabbit replies: Absolutely, twice! First, I ran away from you, and the second time, from the fox.

- What's the difference between a Samogitian and the devil? The devil has patience, but a Samogitian only has his opinion!
- Little Petriukas comes to school with a swollen lip. His friends ask what happened. – We were rowing on the lake with my dad, and a wasp landed on my lip. – Did it bite you? – the friends asked, curious. – No, it didn't have the chance – my dad killed it with the oar.
- A politician is asked: 'How do you sleep at night knowing you're lying to people all day?' He replies: 'Like a baby. I wake up every two hours, cry a little, and then go back to sleep.'
- Three old men are sitting on a bench and talking. The first one says: "My memory isn't what it used to be. I can't even remember what I ate yesterday." The second one says: "Well, I can't even remember what I ate today." The third one says: "I can't even remember who I am or what I'm doing here."

- A countryman invited his friends over. The table was loaded with food. The guests marvel at the spread and ask: "How did you prepare so much food?" The countryman replies: "Well, we're not like city folks who only drink coffee with cookies!"
- A cat and a dog live together. The cat says to the dog, "I'm so beautiful that everyone loves me!" The dog replies, "And I'm so smart, I understand everything!" The cat says, "And I'm so independent, I can sleep all day!" The dog says, "And I'm so loyal, I'm always by my owner's side!" After this conversation, they both decide that they are perfect for each other.

Traits of Lithuanian Humor

Witty and Clever: Lithuanian humor is known for its wit and cleverness. It often involves wordplay and ironic observations, reflecting a deep appreciation for language and social nuances.

Cultural Depth: The humor frequently incorporates cultural references and traditions, offering a rich and engaging perspective on Lithuanian life. It highlights the country's historical and cultural context.

Playful and Reflective: Lithuanian humor balances playful elements with reflective commentary. It provides both entertainment and insight, making it both enjoyable and thought-provoking.

Observational: Lithuanian jokes and anecdotes often involve keen observations about everyday life and social interactions. This observational humor offers a nuanced view of the country's cultural and social dynamics.

Pride and Identity: Humor in Lithuania is often tied to cultural pride and identity. It reflects the country's values and traditions, celebrating its unique characteristics through clever and engaging jokes.

Conclusion

Lithuanian humor offers a distinctive blend of wit and cultural insight, reflecting the country's rich traditions and sharp observational skills. Its clever wordplay and cultural references provide a humorous and engaging perspective on Lithuanian life. Through witty jokes and reflective anecdotes, Lithuanian humor enriches the cultural landscape with its unique and entertaining approach.

Latvia

Latvian Humor: Lively and Observational

Latvian humor is known for its lively and observational nature, capturing the vibrancy of daily life and social interactions in Latvia. This style of humor often combines energetic delivery with sharp observations, reflecting the unique aspects of Latvian culture and society. Latvian jokes and stories frequently draw from everyday experiences, local customs, and the quirks of social behavior, providing a humorous lens through which to view the world.

The liveliness of Latvian humor is often expressed through dynamic storytelling and a playful approach to social commentary. It emphasizes the ability to find humor in various aspects of life, from mundane activities to cultural traditions. Latvian humor is characterized by its warmth and relatability, making it an integral part of social gatherings and casual conversations.

Latvian Jokes and Stories

- At the doctor's office: A Latvian goes to the doctor and says, "Doctor, I think I'm going deaf." The doctor replies, "Can you describe the symptoms?" The Latvian says, "Sure, they're yellow and look like a cat."

- In a restaurant: A Latvian is at a restaurant and orders a steak. When it arrives, it's overcooked. He complains to the waiter, "This steak is so tough, even my dog wouldn't eat it!" The waiter replies, "Well, your dog must be a very picky eater then!"

- Lost in the countryside: A Latvian tourist is lost in the countryside and asks a local for directions. The local says, "Well, if I were you, I wouldn't start from here. But if you're here, just keep going straight until you reach a fork in the road, and then turn left."

- Latvian weather forecast: A Latvian is asked how the weather is today. He replies, "It's perfect for Latvia—raining and windy. Just another day in paradise!"

- The fishing trip: Two Latvians are fishing. One says, "I caught a fish so big, I had to use a crane to lift it!"

The other responds, "That's nothing. I caught a fish so smart, it asked me for directions back to the water!"

- Shopping habits: A Latvian goes to a store and buys only one item. The cashier asks, "Why just one thing?" The Latvian replies, "I'm saving up for a rainy day. You never know when you'll need to buy more!"

- Traditional advice: A Latvian grandmother tells her grandson, "If you ever get lost, just follow the sound of people talking. They'll always lead you to the nearest café or place to rest!"

- A woman complains to her husband, "Our cat always sleeps on my sweater!" The husband suggests, "Maybe you should try knitting a jacket?"

- A man comes home and tells his wife, "Darling, I bought you a new dress!" The wife asks, "What color is it?" The husband replies, "What color? The important thing is that it was cheap!"

- Two Latvians meet. One says to the other, "You know, someone just stole my car!" The other responds, "Well, at least you don't have to worry about anyone stealing it now!"

- A boss tells an employee, "If you keep working so slowly, you'll be fired!" The employee replies, "But I'm doing just fine!" The boss says, "Alright, then work even slower so you can be even better!"

- A Latvian invites a Russian over. The Russian brings a bottle of vodka. The Latvian says, "Thanks, but my fridge is already full!" The Russian replies, "Well, then just give me a glass!"

Traits of Latvian Humor

Lively and Energetic: Latvian humor is characterized by its lively and energetic delivery. It often involves dynamic storytelling and a spirited approach to social commentary.

Observational: The humor frequently includes sharp observations about everyday life and social interactions. It provides a humorous perspective on the nuances of Latvian culture.

Playful and Warm: Latvian humor is playful and warm, emphasizing the joy of shared experiences and the ability to find humor in various aspects of life.

Cultural Reflection: Latvian jokes and stories often incorporate cultural references and local customs, offering a rich and engaging view of Latvian life.

Relatable and Engaging: Humor in Latvia is relatable and engaging, making it an integral part of social interactions and communal gatherings. It fosters a sense of connection and enjoyment.

Conclusion

Latvian humor provides a vibrant and observational view of life in Latvia, capturing the essence of daily experiences and cultural traditions. Its lively delivery and sharp observations offer a humorous and engaging perspective on Latvian society. Through playful jokes and lively stories, Latvian humor enriches the cultural landscape with its unique and entertaining approach.

Estonia

Estonian Humor: Dry and Subtle

Estonian humor is renowned for its dry and subtle nature, reflecting a nuanced approach to comedy that often involves understated wit and quiet irony. This style of humor is characterized by its minimalist delivery and a focus on the small, often overlooked aspects of life. Estonian jokes and anecdotes typically rely on a deep sense of irony and a calm, reflective demeanor, offering a unique and often introspective perspective on social and cultural themes.

The dry humor of Estonia is marked by its restraint and sophistication. It tends to avoid overt exaggeration or loud expressions, instead opting for a more subdued and thought-provoking approach. This subtlety allows Estonian humor to gently highlight the quirks and idiosyncrasies of everyday life, often leaving a lasting impression through its cleverness and elegance.

Estonian Jokes and Anecdotes

- An Estonian is driving in the countryside and sees a sign: "Help us save the environment – don't drive so fast." The Estonian thinks for a moment and says, "Why not? I'll save the environment by driving slower and save on fuel!"

- An Estonian walks into a store and asks the cashier, "Do you have any shoes in my size?" The cashier replies, "Sorry, we don't have any in your size." The Estonian thinks for a moment and says, "Well, then I'll just buy the biggest size you have and wear thick socks!"

- Two Estonians are chatting. One says, "I bought a new car!" The other asks, "What kind is it?" The first one replies, "It's a hybrid!" The other one looks confused and asks, "Is it a hybrid between a car and a tractor?"

- An Estonian goes to a doctor and says, "Doctor, I think I'm getting forgetful." The doctor asks, "When did you first notice it?" The Estonian replies, "When did I first notice what?"

- A tourist asks an Estonian, "How do you deal with the cold winters here?" The Estonian replies, "We just stay inside and complain about the weather."

- An Estonian is asked, "What's the best way to make friends in Estonia?" The Estonian replies, "Just be quiet and wait – people will come to you eventually."

- An Estonian and his friend are hiking in the forest. The friend says, "It's so quiet here, it's eerie." The Estonian replies, "Yes, but it's perfect for thinking about how to fix the fence at home."

Traits of Estonian Humor

Dry and Subtle: Estonian humor is marked by its dry and subtle nature. It relies on understated wit and quiet irony, often delivering humor in a minimalist style.

Irony and Restraint: The humor frequently involves irony and a restrained approach. It avoids overt exaggeration, favoring a more refined and contemplative form of comedy.

Reflective and Sophisticated: Estonian jokes and anecdotes often offer a reflective and sophisticated perspective. They highlight the nuances of life with a calm and thoughtful approach.

Cultural Insight: The humor provides insight into Estonian culture and social dynamics, often using subtle observations to comment on everyday experiences and traditions.

Elegant and Impactful: Despite its understated delivery, Estonian humor can leave a lasting impact. It combines elegance with cleverness, offering a unique and memorable view of life.

Conclusion

Estonian humor offers a distinctive blend of dryness and subtlety, reflecting the country's sophisticated approach to comedy. Its understated wit and ironic observations provide a thoughtful and engaging perspective on Estonian life and culture. Through subtle jokes and reflective anecdotes, Estonian humor enriches the cultural landscape with its unique and elegant style.

Eastern Europe. Resilient and Reflective Humor

Eastern European humor is marked by its sharp wit, irony, and a deep connection to the region's complex history and social dynamics. The humor in Poland, the Czech Republic, and Slovakia often reflects a blend of resilience, satire, and a playful engagement with the quirks of daily life and historical experiences.

Poland

Polish Humor: Resilient and Ironic

Polish humor is celebrated for its resilience and ironic flair, reflecting a deep tradition of using humor to navigate and comment on the complexities of life. This style of humor often combines a sharp wit with a resilient spirit, showcasing the ability of Poles to find humor in challenging situations. Polish jokes and stories frequently involve irony and clever observations, providing a humorous yet insightful perspective on various aspects of Polish society.

The resilience in Polish humor stems from a historical backdrop of overcoming adversity, with humor serving as a coping mechanism and a means of solidarity. This irony is often used to critique societal norms and political realities, offering a way to address serious issues through a humorous lens. Polish humor is characterized by its ability to balance sharpness with warmth, making it both engaging and thought-provoking.

Popular Polish Jokes and Stories

- A Polish man walks into a shop and asks for a dozen eggs. The shopkeeper gives him the eggs and says, "That will be 12 zlotys." The man replies, "What a deal! I'll take two dozen."

- A Polish farmer is asked why he's always late to town. He replies, "I'm not late; I'm just on Polish time." When asked what that means, he says, "It means I arrive exactly when I plan to, not when everyone else thinks I should."

- An American tourist asks a Polish man, "What's the secret to Polish cuisine?" The Polish man replies, "Simple – add a little bit of garlic and hope for the best."

- A Polish student tells his teacher, "I'm going to be an astronaut!" The teacher asks, "Really? How do you plan to get there?" The student replies, "I'll take a very long vacation and hope for a free ride."

- A Polish grandmother is asked about her secret to living a long life. She replies, "Don't worry about the little things – just enjoy the big moments, like when your grandkids visit and bring you sweets!"

- Two Polish friends are discussing their weekend plans. One says, "I'm going to the countryside to relax." The other asks, "How will you relax?" The first replies, "By not doing anything and pretending the world outside doesn't exist."

- A Polish man is trying to fix his broken car. A neighbor asks, "Can I help you?" The Polish man replies, "No thanks, I'm trying to figure out if I can fix it with just duct tape and good intentions."

Traits of Polish Humor

Resilient and Ironic: Polish humor is characterized by its resilience and ironic perspective. It reflects the ability to find humor in adversity and use irony to address societal and personal issues.

Clever and Observational: The humor often involves clever observations and sharp wit. It provides insightful commentary on everyday life and social dynamics.

Coping Mechanism: Humor serves as a coping mechanism in Poland, helping people manage stress and navigate difficult situations with a positive outlook.

Cultural Reflection: Polish jokes and stories frequently incorporate cultural and historical references, offering a rich and engaging view of Polish life and traditions.

Warm and Engaging: Despite its ironic edge, Polish humor maintains a sense of warmth and engagement. It fosters a sense of connection and shared understanding through its clever and reflective nature.

Conclusion

Polish humor offers a distinctive blend of resilience and irony, reflecting the country's ability to navigate and comment on life's complexities with wit and cleverness. Its sharp observations and humorous perspective provide valuable insights into Polish culture and society. Through engaging jokes and thoughtful anecdotes, Polish humor enriches the cultural landscape with its unique and reflective approach.

Czech Republic

Czech Humor: Witty and Satirical

Czech humor is renowned for its wit and satirical edge, reflecting a tradition of clever commentary and incisive observation. This style of humor often combines sharp wit with a satirical approach, allowing Czechs to explore and critique social, political, and cultural issues through a humorous lens. Czech jokes and anecdotes are characterized by their ability to provide insightful reflections on various aspects of life, while also entertaining and engaging the audience.

The satirical nature of Czech humor often involves a playful yet critical examination of societal norms and political realities. It uses humor as a tool to question and challenge, offering both entertainment and a means of engaging with deeper issues. Czech humor is known for its cleverness and sophistication, making it a distinctive feature of the country's cultural landscape.

Czech Jokes and Anecdotes

- A man walks into a store and asks the shopkeeper, "Do you sell 'Budweiser' beer?" The shopkeeper replies, "Yes, we do. But it's a bit pricey!" The man responds, "That's okay, I'm just looking for something to make me forget my problems. What's your most expensive beer?"

- A Czech man and a Slovak man are arguing about who has the better beer. The Czech says, "Our beer is so good that it's almost like drinking happiness!" The Slovak replies, "In that case, your beer must be so strong that it makes you forget all your problems, even if it's just for a moment!"

- A man says to his friend, "I went to a fortune teller, and she told me I would be poor and lonely." His friend asks, "So what did you do?" The man replies, "I went to another fortune teller, and she told me the same thing! Now I'm just trying to be optimistic."

- A Czech woman goes to a doctor and says, "Doctor, I have a problem. I can't sleep." The doctor asks, "How long have you had this problem?" The woman replies, "Since I started counting sheep." The doctor says, "Well, stop counting sheep and start counting your blessings!"

- A man is walking through a Czech village when he sees a sign that says, "Talking Dog for Sale." He rings the bell, and the owner says, "The dog is in the backyard." The man walks into the backyard and asks the dog, "Can you talk?" The dog replies, "Yep." The man asks, "So, what's your story?" The dog looks up and says, "Well, I discovered that I could talk when I was young. I wanted to help the government, so I told them about my ability. In no time, they had me traveling around the world, telling people about my talents. I've had a great life!" The man is amazed. He asks the owner, "How much do you want for the dog?" The owner says, "Ten dollars." The man exclaims, "Ten dollars? This dog is amazing! Why on earth are you selling him so cheap?" The owner replies, "Because he's a liar. He didn't do any of that stuff."

- A Czech man is driving his car when he gets stopped by a policeman. The officer says, "Do you know how fast you were going?" The man replies, "No, but I know exactly how slow I'm going now!"

- A Czech teacher asks her students, "What is the difference between a lawyer and a herd of cows?" One student replies, "I don't know." The teacher says, "Well, a herd of cows can be easily found, but a lawyer is hard to find!"

Traits of Czech Humor

Witty and Satirical: Czech humor is known for its wit and satirical approach. It involves clever commentary and critical reflections on social and political issues.

Clever Observations: The humor often includes sharp observations and insightful critiques. It provides a sophisticated and engaging perspective on various aspects of life.

Critical and Reflective: Czech humor frequently uses satire to address and question societal norms and political realities. It serves as both entertainment and a means of exploring deeper issues.

Cultural Insight: Czech jokes and anecdotes often incorporate cultural and historical references, offering a rich view of Czech life and traditions through a humorous lens.

Engaging and Entertaining: Despite its critical edge, Czech humor remains engaging and entertaining. It fosters a sense of connection and provides a thoughtful yet enjoyable perspective.

Conclusion

Czech humor offers a distinctive blend of wit and satire, reflecting the country's tradition of clever commentary and insightful observation. Its sharp, engaging jokes and reflective anecdotes provide a unique perspective on Czech society and culture. Through its sophisticated and entertaining approach, Czech humor enriches the cultural landscape with its thoughtful and entertaining style.

Slovakia

Slovak Humor: Straightforward and Witty

Slovak humor is characterized by its straightforwardness and wit, reflecting a direct and engaging approach to comedy. This style of humor often involves clear, simple delivery and a sharp, clever edge, making it both accessible and entertaining. Slovak jokes and stories are known for their ability to capture the essence of everyday life with a humorous and often insightful perspective.

The straightforward nature of Slovak humor makes it easy to relate to, while its witty elements add a layer of sophistication. This combination allows Slovaks to address various aspects of life, from mundane experiences to social observations, with a refreshing sense of clarity and humor. Slovak humor is often direct yet clever, offering both amusement and reflection through its engaging style.

Slovak Jokes and Stories

- A Slovak man is sitting at a bar, enjoying a drink. He notices a sign that says, "Free Beer Tomorrow."

Curious, he asks the bartender, "When is the free beer available?" The bartender replies, "Tomorrow." The man then asks, "But today?" The bartender responds, "Today you pay for your beer!"

- A Slovak woman goes to the doctor and complains, "Doctor, my husband and I haven't been getting along. He's always complaining that I talk too much!" The doctor looks at her and says, "Well, maybe you should talk less." The woman replies, "That's what he said, but I don't understand how talking less will help. I need to talk more to work things out!"

- A Slovak farmer is asked by his friend how his farm is doing. The farmer replies, "Oh, it's going well. I planted a new field of potatoes this year." The friend asks, "How much did you plant?" The farmer responds, "About 50 kilograms." The friend is surprised and asks, "That's a lot of potatoes! What will you do with them?" The farmer replies, "I'm not sure, but at least I won't have to buy potatoes for a while!"

- A Slovak man is in a store and sees a sign that says, "Free Coffee." He asks the store clerk, "Where can I get the free coffee?" The clerk replies, "You can get it after you make a purchase." The man asks, "How much do I need to spend?" The clerk responds, "Just enough to buy a cup of coffee!"

- A Slovak student is asked by his teacher, "What is the capital of Slovakia?" The student replies, "Bratislava." The teacher then asks, "And what is the capital of the Czech Republic?" The student thinks for a moment and says, "Prague." The teacher smiles and says, "Very good! Now, what is the capital of Hungary?" The student responds, "Budapest." The teacher nods and says, "Great! You've done very well today. Keep up the good work!" The student replies, "Thank you! I hope I can remember all these capitals in the future."

- A Slovak man is driving his car when he notices a sign that says, "No Parking." He thinks, "What's the harm in parking here for just a few minutes?" So, he parks his car and goes into a store. When he comes back, he finds a ticket on his windshield. He looks at the ticket and says, "Well, at least the parking was free!"

- A Slovak man goes to a job interview and is asked, "Why do you want to work for this company?" The man replies, "I want to work here because I heard the pay is good." The interviewer asks, "And what else?" The man responds, "And because I want to make a good impression." The interviewer smiles and says, "Well, if you can make a good impression and get the job, you'll be a great addition to our team!"

Traits of Slovak Humor

Straightforward and Direct: Slovak humor is characterized by its straightforward and direct approach. It delivers jokes and stories with clarity and simplicity, making it easily accessible.

Witty and Clever: The humor often includes witty observations and clever remarks. It adds a layer of sophistication to the straightforward delivery, enhancing the comedic effect.

Relatable and Engaging: Slovak jokes and stories are relatable and engaging. They capture the essence of everyday experiences and social interactions with a humorous twist.

Cultural Insight: Slovak humor frequently incorporates cultural references and local customs, offering a rich and engaging view of Slovak life and traditions.

Amusing and Reflective: Despite its directness, Slovak humor is both amusing and reflective. It provides entertainment while also offering thoughtful commentary on various aspects of life.

Conclusion

Slovak humor offers a distinctive blend of straightforwardness and wit, reflecting the country's direct and engaging approach to comedy. Its clear delivery and clever observations provide an entertaining and insightful view of Slovak society and culture. Through its relatable jokes and engaging stories, Slovak humor enriches the cultural landscape with its unique and enjoyable style.

Central Europe. Intellectual and Playful Humor

Central European humor, found in Austria, Switzerland, and Hungary, is marked by its sophistication and subtlety, often laced with a hint of absurdity. In Austria, humor frequently intertwines with the country's rich cultural and intellectual traditions, providing a blend of sharp wit and playful commentary that reflects the depth of Austrian social and artistic life. Similarly, in Switzerland, humor tends to be nuanced and often relies on clever wordplay and cultural references, reflecting the country's diverse linguistic and cultural landscape.

Hungary contributes its own flavor of humor, characterized by a sharp intellect and a playful spirit that often delves into social and political satire. Hungarian humor skillfully balances insightful observations with a sense of whimsy, offering a unique perspective on both daily life and broader societal issues. Across Central Europe, humor serves not only as entertainment but also as a means of engaging with and reflecting on the region's rich heritage and intellectual traditions.

Austria

Austrian Humor: Sophisticated and Subtle

Austrian humor is distinguished by its sophistication and subtlety, reflecting a refined and nuanced approach to comedy. This style of humor often involves a delicate balance between wit and understatement, showcasing a deep appreciation for the nuances of social and cultural commentary. Austrian jokes and cultural observations frequently employ a subtle form of satire and irony, offering a sophisticated perspective on various aspects of life in Austria.

The subtlety of Austrian humor is evident in its ability to deliver clever observations with a gentle touch. This approach allows for a more refined and contemplative form of comedy, often engaging with complex ideas and cultural nuances. Austrian humor is known for its ability to blend elegance with insight, providing a unique and thoughtful view of Austrian society and traditions.

Austrian Jokes and Cultural Observations

- An Austrian man walks into a bakery and asks for a loaf of bread. The baker hands him a fresh loaf and says, "That'll be 3 euros." The man looks at the bread and says, "I could get this cheaper in Germany!" The baker smiles and replies, "Yes, but in Austria, you get to enjoy it fresh and warm!"

- A tourist in Vienna asks an Austrian local, "What's the best way to get to the Schönbrunn Palace?" The local replies, "Well, you could take the tram or the bus, but the best way is to ask for directions from someone who's been lost in Vienna before. They'll know all the shortcuts!"

- An Austrian and a Swiss are discussing their countries' different approaches to punctuality. The Austrian says, "In Austria, we pride ourselves on being on time." The Swiss replies, "In Switzerland, we're so punctual that we even arrive early!" The Austrian laughs and says, "Yes, but at least in Austria, we know how to enjoy the wait!"

- A Viennese man is asked by a friend, "What's the secret to a happy marriage?" The man replies, "Simple! Always agree with your wife, even when you're wrong. That way, you're never really wrong!"

- An Austrian farmer is showing his new tractor to a neighbor. The neighbor asks, "How much did it cost?" The farmer replies, "Oh, it cost a fortune, but it's worth it. Now, I can plow my fields faster and have more time to enjoy my beer!"

- A Vienna restaurant owner is asked, "What's the best way to describe Austrian cuisine?" The owner responds, "It's simple and hearty. We believe in using only the freshest ingredients and serving them with a side of good conversation."

- An Austrian and a German are talking about their favorite beers. The Austrian says, "In Austria, we have the best beer in the world." The German replies, "Oh, we have great beer too, but we like to drink it in moderation." The Austrian smiles and says, "Well, we like to drink it in good company – moderation is optional!"

Traits of Austrian Humor

Sophisticated and Subtle: Austrian humor is characterized by its sophistication and subtlety. It often involves refined wit and gentle irony, delivering humor with a delicate touch.

Elegant and Reflective: The humor frequently incorporates elegance and reflective observations. It engages with cultural nuances and social dynamics in a thoughtful manner.

Cultural Insight: Austrian jokes and observations often include cultural and historical references, offering a rich and engaging view of Austrian life and traditions through a subtle lens.

Clever and Thoughtful: The humor combines cleverness with thoughtfulness. It provides insightful commentary on various aspects of life while maintaining a refined and understated approach.

Meaningful and Enjoyable: Despite its subtlety, Austrian humor remains meaningful and enjoyable. It enriches the cultural landscape with its unique and sophisticated style.

Conclusion

Austrian humor offers a distinctive blend of sophistication and subtlety, reflecting the country's refined approach to comedy. Its elegant and thoughtful observations provide a unique perspective on Austrian society and culture. Through its subtle wit and insightful jokes, Austrian humor enriches the cultural landscape with its sophisticated and engaging style.

Switzerland

Swiss Humor: Neutral, Yet Sharp

Swiss humor is characterized by its subtlety, precision, and often a touch of dry wit. It reflects the country's reputation for efficiency and orderliness, while also embracing the cultural diversity and regional quirks of its multilingual population. Swiss jokes often play on the contrasts between the country's diverse linguistic and cultural regions, offering a humorous look at the coexistence of multiple languages and traditions.

Swiss Jokes

- A Swiss tourist asks a local, "What's the best way to experience Switzerland?" The local replies, "Oh, that's easy. Just visit the Alps, eat some fondue, and complain about the weather – it's a complete Swiss experience!"

- A Swiss man is asked about his country's strict punctuality. He replies, "In Switzerland, even the trains are punctual. If they're late, it's a national emergency!"

- An American tourist is visiting Switzerland and asks a Swiss guide, "Why are Swiss watches so precise?" The guide responds, "Because in Switzerland, even time is taken seriously. We've never seen a late watch here – it's simply unheard of!"

- A Swiss banker is talking to a foreign client about Swiss banking secrecy. The client asks, "How secure is my money in a Swiss bank?" The banker replies, "It's so secure that even we don't know where it is!"

- A Swiss and a German are discussing their countries' food. The Swiss says, "In Switzerland, we make the best cheese." The German replies, "Yes, but we have great sausages too!" The Swiss smiles and says, "True, but our cheese has been known to bring people together – it's a real Swiss unifier!"

- A Swiss woman tells her friend, "My husband always complains about our house being too small." Her friend replies, "Why don't you move to a bigger place?" The woman says, "Oh, we could, but then we'd have to clean more, and we'd miss our cozy little home."

- A Swiss man is asked why his country is so clean. He replies, "It's simple. We're all very conscious of our environment and have a great respect for cleanliness. Plus, we have a saying: 'If you drop something, pick it up – it's good for the soul!'"

Traits of Swiss Humor

Subtlety and Precision: Swiss humor is often characterized by its subtlety and precision. Jokes may involve clever wordplay and a refined sense of timing, reflecting the country's emphasis on orderliness and efficiency.

Multicultural Influences: The humor reflects Switzerland's multicultural and multilingual environment. Jokes often play on the contrasts and interactions between the country's various linguistic and cultural groups.

Dry Wit: Swiss humor frequently involves a touch of dry wit. The jokes are often understated, with a focus on the cleverness of the punchline rather than overt expressiveness.

Orderliness and Efficiency: Swiss humor often mirrors the country's values of orderliness and efficiency. Jokes may involve precise observations and a structured approach to humor.

Playful Contrasts: Swiss humor often highlights the playful contrasts between different aspects of Swiss life, from regional differences to the juxtaposition of tradition and modernity.

How Swiss Humor Differs

Swiss humor is distinct for its subtlety and precision, reflecting the country's cultural values of orderliness and efficiency. Unlike more overt forms of comedy, Swiss jokes often involve dry wit and clever wordplay, offering a refined and nuanced perspective on life.

The humor also embraces the multicultural and multilingual nature of Switzerland, providing a unique look at the interactions and contrasts within the country. It combines a sense of precision with playful contrasts, creating a distinctive and engaging comedic style.

Hungary

Hungarian Humor: Rich and Flavorful

Hungarian humor is known for its rich and flavorful qualities, reflecting a vibrant tradition of comedy that combines wit with a deep cultural resonance. This style of humor often involves elaborate storytelling, clever wordplay, and a unique blend of cultural references. Hungarian jokes and observations provide a colorful and engaging perspective on various aspects of life, showcasing a distinctive blend of humor that is both entertaining and deeply rooted in Hungarian culture.

The richness of Hungarian humor can be seen in its use of vivid language and intricate narratives. It often draws on historical, cultural, and social themes, presenting them with a humorous twist that highlights the complexities of Hungarian life. Hungarian humor is characterized by its ability to convey deep cultural insights through a playful and imaginative approach, making it a significant aspect of the country's cultural heritage.

Hungarian Jokes and Observations

- A Hungarian man goes to a doctor and says, "Doctor, I have a problem. My wife is always trying to control everything in the house!" The doctor replies, "That's not a problem, that's just Hungarian!"

- A tourist in Hungary asks a local, "What's the best way to experience Hungarian cuisine?" The local replies, "Easy! Just order goulash. It's so hearty you'll feel like a Hungarian in no time!"

- A Hungarian is bragging about his country's wine. He says, "In Hungary, we have the best wine in the world!" A foreigner asks, "How do you know?" The Hungarian replies, "Well, we've been making it for centuries, and the best way to taste history is to drink it!"

- A Hungarian student is asked why he is always late to class. He says, "In Hungary, we have a saying: 'Better late than never,' but I like to take it to the extreme!"

- A Hungarian and a Romanian are having a friendly debate about their national dishes. The Romanian says, "Our dishes are delicious and varied!" The Hungarian replies, "True, but we have goulash – it's like having the entire kitchen in one pot!"

- A Hungarian is explaining why he doesn't like to travel. He says, "Why would I leave Hungary? We have everything here – great food, great wine, and the best company!"

- A Hungarian man is telling a joke about his family: "My family is so Hungarian that when we sit down for a meal, even the tablecloth is full of stories!"

Traits of Hungarian Humor

Rich and Flavorful: Hungarian humor is characterized by its richness and flavor. It involves elaborate storytelling, clever wordplay, and vibrant cultural references.

Playful and Engaging: The humor is often playful and engaging, drawing on a deep cultural heritage to entertain and amuse. It uses imaginative narratives and vivid language.

Cultural Insight: Hungarian jokes and observations frequently incorporate cultural and historical themes, offering a colorful and insightful view of Hungarian life.

Clever and Narrative: The humor combines cleverness with narrative depth. It presents cultural insights and social observations through elaborate and entertaining stories.

Vibrant and Joyful: Despite its complexity, Hungarian humor remains vibrant and joyful. It enriches the cultural landscape with its unique and engaging style.

Conclusion

Hungarian humor offers a distinctive blend of richness and flavor, reflecting the country's vibrant tradition of comedy. Its elaborate storytelling and clever observations provide a colorful and engaging perspective on Hungarian society and culture. Through its playful and imaginative approach, Hungarian humor enriches the cultural landscape with its unique and flavorful style.

Conclusion

Summary of European Humor Styles

Throughout our exploration of European humor, we have encountered a rich tapestry of comedic styles that reflect the diverse cultural landscapes of the continent. From the dry and subtle wit of Scandinavia to the rich and flavorful storytelling of Hungary, each European country brings its unique flavor to the world of humor. We have seen how humor varies widely, from the sharp and satirical observations of the Czech Republic to the sophisticated and subtle jokes of Austria.

In Denmark and Sweden, humor often manifests as playful and observational, while in Norway and Finland, it leans towards minimalism and dry wit. The humor in Belgium and Switzerland showcases a multilingual and diverse character, reflecting their complex cultural contexts. The distinctiveness of humor in Eastern Europe, with countries like Poland and Slovakia, demonstrates a blend of resilience and straightforwardness. Meanwhile, the humor of the Baltic States, including Lithuania, Latvia, and Estonia, highlights a mix of cultural insights and dry wit.

The Balkans present a tapestry of rich and varied humor, while Central Europe, encompassing Austria, Switzerland, and Hungary, offers a sophisticated and flavorful perspective. Finally, the diverse humor of Greece, Serbia, and Croatia, along with the unique perspectives of Germany and Denmark, rounds out our exploration of Europe's humor.

The Role of Humor in Bridging Cultures

Humor plays a crucial role in bridging cultural divides and fostering understanding across different societies. It serves as a universal language that transcends borders, allowing people from diverse backgrounds to connect and share experiences. By engaging with humor from various European cultures, we gain insight into the values, traditions, and social dynamics that shape each society.

Humor not only entertains but also acts as a powerful tool for breaking down cultural barriers. It offers a means to address sensitive topics, critique societal norms, and explore shared human experiences in a way that is both approachable and engaging. Through laughter and wit, humor creates opportunities for cross-cultural dialogue and mutual appreciation, helping to build bridges between different cultures.

Final Thoughts on Humor Across Europe

As we conclude our journey through European humor, it is clear that humor is a vital and multifaceted aspect of life across the continent. Each country's comedic style offers a glimpse into its cultural identity and societal values, revealing the rich diversity and complexity of European life.

From the understated elegance of Austrian humor to the playful and rich storytelling of Hungary, European humor enriches our understanding of the continent's cultural fabric. It reminds us of the shared human experience of finding joy and laughter in everyday life, despite our differences.

Ultimately, humor serves as a testament to the creativity and resilience of people across Europe. It celebrates the unique qualities of each culture while highlighting the common threads that unite us all. By embracing the humor of Europe, we gain not only entertainment but also a deeper appreciation for the diverse and vibrant cultures that make up this remarkable continent.

Thank You

Thank you for joining us on this humorous journey across Europe! If you enjoyed discovering the diverse and vibrant humor of different European cultures, we would greatly appreciate your support. Please consider leaving a positive review on Amazon. Your feedback not only helps other readers find and appreciate this book but also encourages us to continue exploring and sharing the rich tapestry of European humor. Your support means a lot to us!

Witty Wanderer

Printed in Great Britain
by Amazon